Contents

Preface

This book — part of a new series, *From Reading Research to Practice* — is designed to bring to those working in the field of reading and literacy the most significant research underlying effective practices in reading instruction. Written for teachers of reading, this series will also be a valuable resource for prospective teachers, administrators, and researchers who seek to understand the new as well as the enduring research in the teaching of reading.

The reading field has come to expect that the reading of children who lag behind during the first few grades can be significantly improved with good instruction. Similar confidence in treating the reading difficulties of adolescents has not been common. Indeed, the general consensus has been that even when treated, the poor reading of adolescents does not improve appreciably.

Mary Beth Curtis and Ann Marie Longo take a different view. In this book, they present a remedial program for adolescents who are behind in reading as much as five to six grade levels. With this program, students make impressive gains in reading of about two years for every year of instruction; thus, it is possible to bring most of them up to grade level. The program, based on research and practice in reading and reading disabilities, has great simplicity, and does not require elaborate and expensive teacher training.

Developed at Boys Town Reading Center and replicated in affiliated public schools, the program has great promise for adolescents who do not read well enough to continue their education or for the requirements of today's workplace.

Jeanne S. Chall, Ph.D., *Series Editor*
John F. Onofrey, *Editor*

Introduction

When most people think of Boys Town, they think of Mickey Rooney or Spencer Tracy, or maybe even the phrase, "He ain't heavy, Father ... he's m' brother." But the Boys Town of today differs in many ways from the one founded by Father Flanagan in 1917. In addition to the original long-term, residential-care facility, Boys Town has become a national leader in the development of cutting-edge programs to help children, families, schools, and other child-care providers. In 1996, Boys Town provided direct care for more than 29,000 children, assisted more than 377,000 children and families through its national hotline, and affected more than 750,000 children and families through its outreach and training programs.

Among Boys Town's services is its Reading Center, a laboratory for older adolescents with reading problems. Established in 1990, the goals of the Reading Center are to develop research-based programs that prove effective in Boys Town's schools and to disseminate the programs to other schools around the country. Toward these goals, the Reading Center has developed a reading curriculum that is designed to accelerate reading growth in at-risk adolescents. Our purpose in this book is to describe the methods and materials that make up that curriculum, along with the research and experiences that led us to design it the way that we did.

Although boys and girls typically come to Boys Town two to three years behind in reading, some are reading as many as five to six years below grade level. We needed a curriculum that would help students at several different points along a continuum of reading development, ranging from the ability to identify words in print, all the way up to the ability to analyze what is read and to use reading as a way to acquire new concepts and points of view. We also needed a curriculum that would result in accelerated growth in a relatively short period of time.

Prior to coming to Boys Town, we both had worked in the Harvard Reading Laboratory, where individuals ranging from 7 to 50 years of age came for help with their reading problems. Based on that experience, we knew our curriculum had to have a developmental framework, and also meet students' needs by building on their strengths. We also knew that it would be particularly important for our teaching materials and techniques to be appealing to our audience of young adults.

Since our goal was to develop a reading curriculum that could be disseminated nationwide, we needed to keep costs in mind. Because few high schools have the funds necessary to support individual tutorials, our instruction needed to be effective with groups. Aside from money, though, we had another very important reason for wanting to extend the principles of one-to-one instruction to groups. For young adults with reading difficulties, inappropriate classroom behaviors can often contribute to academic failure. By working in groups, we knew, teens could benefit from the opportunity to learn and practice social skills at the same time that they were improving their skills in reading.[1]

In this book, we discuss the theory, research, methods, and materials that form the basis for our reading program in more detail. We begin by presenting some of the causes and consequences of reading problems in adolescents in Chapter 1. Chapter 2 contains a developmental approach for understanding reading difficulties, and Chapter 3 describes a process for identifying students' strengths and needs in reading. In Chapter 4, we review the components of effective reading instruction.

Chapter 5 contains some recommendations for remediating problems in word identification; in Chapter 6, we describe an effective approach for vocabulary instruction. Chapter 7 focuses on methods and materials for teaching comprehension. In Chapter 8, we make some recommendations about evaluating and communicating students' growth in reading achievement. Chapter 9 contains some guidelines for classroom management, and in Chapter 10, we summarize the principles that make the program work.

Concern about illiteracy abounds. Solutions are more difficult to find. Indeed, in many circles, reading failure in older adolescents is viewed as failure too late to overcome. The Boys Town Reading Curriculum is a program that has successfully reversed reading failure in at-risk youth. The program would not have been possible without the cooperation and help of the teachers and students for whom it is designed. This is what really makes the curriculum work. It has been developed and refined in high school classrooms across the country, keeping us continually aware of the needs of the students and teachers we are seeking to help. To those teachers and students, we owe special thanks.

---

[1] See Connolly et al. (1995) for a description of how this is done.

Chapter 1

Reading Problems in Adolescents: Causes and Consequences

On her first day at Boys Town High School, Sheila told one of her teachers, "I have a lot of problems to work on. At first I didn't want help, but now I do ... I would like for me to make some changes in my life."[2]

Only 15 years old at the time, Sheila did seem to have more than her share of difficulties. She had been in jail for four months prior to coming to Boys Town. In addition to chronic academic failure, she had a history of physical assaults on peers, along with numerous instances of rebellion against authority. According to Sheila, reading was one of her favorite subjects in school. But when asked to read aloud, Sheila's problems became evident with materials written at the fifth-grade level. As she came across more and more words that she was unable to read, she began to scowl. Soon after, she looked away from the page, tossed the materials on the table, and announced, "I don't feel like reading right now."

When he was 16 years old, Phil was given the following choice by a judge: serve six months in lockup for vandalism and theft, or go to Boys Town for 18 months. Phil chose Boys Town, saying upon his arrival, "I can't get along with my parents. I get mad very easy. I would like to learn how to control my temper." Phil was quick to note that reading was one of his least favorite activities. When asked to complete the following statement, "I'd rather read than ...," he paused only briefly before responding "die." Even so, when requested to read, he was cooperative and pleasant. He read very slowly and laboriously, though, and was able to get very little from the content of materials written beyond a fourth-grade level of difficulty.

Every secondary level teacher knows a Sheila or a Phil. Difficulties in reading and behavior problems seem to go hand in hand, particularly in older

---

[2] The students described in this book are real; their names have been changed to assure anonymity.

students.[3] But how and why did troubled teens end up with reading problems in the first place? Can reading failure as great as Sheila's and Phil's be overcome? Does it make sense, in terms of the time and the money required, to even try?

The Reading Center at Boys Town was founded in 1990 with the mission of finding the answers to questions like these. In this book, we share some of our findings.

For more than 80 years, Boys Town (officially known as Father Flanagan's Boys' Home) has been providing care and treatment for children who are emotionally and socially at risk because of factors such as school failure, broken homes, chronic neglect and abuse, and illegal and antisocial behaviors. Located at the Home's national headquarters in the Village of Boys Town, Nebraska, the Reading Center is an applied research and development facility. The village is also home to Boys Town's largest residential and educational site, where annually, about 850 youth are in residence. The average age of youth at the home campus is 15 years, with a range from 8 to 18 years. About 60% of the students are Caucasian, 25% African American, 10% Latino, and 3% Native American. About 40% are female. At any given time, children from 30 to 40 states are residents at Boys Town. Youth live together in groups of six to eight with trained married couples who guide and instruct them on a 24-hour basis. At the two schools on campus — a middle school and a high school — students are provided academic opportunities as well as job and independent living skills.

For the 300 or so youth who arrive at Boys Town's Home Campus every year, reading achievement typically lags two to three years behind these students' grade placement in school. At the Reading Center, our goal is twofold: to help Boys Town students to improve their reading skills, and to disseminate instructional programs found effective in our schools to schools around the country.

As part of our work, we have looked at the case files of students who come to us with reading difficulties to see whether there are any clues about how and why reading problems develop.[4]

For students with the most severe reading problems (i.e., their reading

---

3 Poor school achievement is one of the best predictors of later delinquency and criminal behavior (Kellermann, Fuqua-Whitley, & Rivara, 1996). See also Cornwall and Bawden (1992) and Hinshaw (1992) for reviews of research on the correlation between behavior problems and problems in reading.

4 Beth Chmelka, a Research Assistant at the Reading Center, read the case files, designed the coding scheme, and did the analyses for this research project.

achievement is five to six years below grade level), difficulty in reading is typically first noted in their educational records at about age 11, two years *after* the age at which problems in their behavior were first noticed. This may be why only about 10 to 15% of our incoming youth have been identified as students with learning disabilities. By the time the children's lack of progress in learning to read was recognized, many of them were already classified as students with behavior disorders or emotional disturbances.

In about half of the cases of students with more moderate reading problems (i.e., two to three years below grade level), difficulty in reading is not even noted in their files. When moderate reading problems are noticed, students' ages at time of identification tend to be around 14 years, more than three years after recognition of their behavior problems.

The younger the students were when someone first noted a reading problem in their files, the greater the severity of their behavior problems at the time of admission to Boys Town.

Boys Town youth with reading problems do not come from families that are more dysfunctional than the families of youth without reading difficulties. However, the earlier a difficulty in reading is noted, the more likely it is that the child's family has mental health issues and poor communication skills at the time of the youth's admission. Moreover, we find that the families of youth with more severe reading problems are more likely to be abusing alcohol or drugs than families of youth with less severe reading problems. Parents of youth with more severe reading problems also are more likely to be experiencing economic difficulties (e.g., unemployment, financial problems) than parents of youth with less severe reading problems.

Boys Town youth with reading problems have lower IQ scores than youth who are not experiencing any reading difficulty (88 vs. 96). Also, youth with more severe reading problems have lower IQ scores than youth with more moderate reading difficulties (84 vs. 92). Since the average age of our students is 15 years, these IQ differences are difficult to interpret. On the one hand, an IQ score is the most commonly used measure for estimating reading potential. On the other hand, being able to read affects one's ability to acquire the kinds of information assessed on an IQ test. In other words, IQ differences among older adolescents may result from actual differences in the potential for learning to read. But they may also result from the impact that reading problems and related school problems can have on growth in measured intelligence.

All in all, what have we learned from analyzing our students' case histories? Perhaps our most important finding is the following: Unraveling how and why troubled teens ended up with reading problems in the first place is a difficult, if not impossible, task. Fortunately, for all concerned, we also have conducted research that clearly demonstrates that it is not necessary to identify the underlying causes of a student's reading problem in order to help. What is required is an understanding of how reading develops, and how a developmental approach to reading instruction can be applied to produce accelerated growth.

A more detailed explanation of how a developmental approach to understanding reading difficulties in adolescence works is described in the next chapter.

Chapter 2

A Developmental Approach to Understanding Reading Difficulties

How can teachers best help teens to become better readers? The answer lies in understanding where students are in terms of their reading development.

Some adolescents can become better readers by simply giving them more time for reading, more encouragement, and more stimulating materials to read. The term *aliterate* is probably the best way to describe this group of students. In spite of being fairly capable readers, they do not engage in reading. Reading bores them, they will tell you, and they see very little purpose in doing it.

With these students, our job as teachers is to help them get into the habit of reading, so that their reading skills will not begin to deteriorate from lack of use. Ensuring that students view their teachers as active and involved readers, making time for teachers to read aloud and conduct book talks in class, and providing opportunities for sustained silent reading — all are ways to create an environment that will be conducive to literacy.[5]

For far too many other adolescents, however, time and encouragement will never be enough. The term *functional illiteracy* best describes their plight. They are unable to use reading with facility in their everyday lives. Reading frustrates them and often triggers disruptive behavior. Improvement for them will result only from direct instruction in the processes, knowledge, and skills they have not yet had the opportunity to acquire.

Adolescents like these have been the focus of our work at the Reading Center, and they are the group we are concerned with in this book.

To design an effective program that will help older students who need direct instruction, the first step involves selecting a framework that is grounded in theory and research. The framework we chose to guide our instructional design was Jeanne Chall's stages of reading development.[6]

---

5 See Allen (1995) for suggestions for materials, approaches, and techniques for aliterate teens.

According to Chall, acquisition of skill in reading is a process that takes place gradually, not something that occurs overnight. As children learn to read they go through several distinct stages of reading development, spanning a period of time from birth through adulthood.

At Boys Town, our students' average length of stay is 18 to 22 months, not 18 to 22 years! Given that, why did we select such a comprehensive scheme for our theoretical base? There were two reasons. First, our teaching experiences and knowledge of available research convinced us that, regardless of age, learning to read involves a core set of knowledge and skills. Second, as we came to know our students better, we recognized that their reading skills were at several different levels of development.

Chall describes six distinct stages of reading development:

Stage 0/Prereading: Readers in this first stage of development are able to "say back" materials that have been read to them repeatedly. Although they are not really reading yet — in the sense of identifying words on the page — they are able to engage in this "pretend reading" of books because they understand that books have meaning. They also know that groups of letters written on a page stand for words.

Very few of the adolescents with whom we work are experiencing any difficulty at this stage of reading development. Most can read some words, albeit at a very low level of difficulty (e.g., *book, no, jump, come*), and they are able to recognize words they encounter in their environment (e.g., *STOP, Reebok, Coke*).

Stage 1/Decoding: This stage — when actual reading begins — is where our students begin to experience difficulties. Readers in this stage are beginning to associate letters with sounds, and spoken words with printed ones. Because they are still in the process of acquiring skill in "sounding out" words, though, Stage 1 readers are able to read only a fraction of the words whose meanings they know.

About one out of ten older adolescents that we work with is struggling with this stage of development. For many of them, the difficulty is compounded by their tendency to abandon the process of trying to decode an unknown word and instead guess at the word based on the context of what they are reading. Hence, teaching older adolescents at this stage of reading develop-

---

[6] A more complete description of Jeanne Chall's theory can be found in *Stages of Reading Development* (1983, 1996).

ment usually involves two steps: first, providing direct instruction in letter-sound correspondences, and second, providing a great deal of encouragement and multiple opportunities to apply the decoding skills once they have been acquired. The instructional materials used to teach adolescents at this stage of development also need to be selected carefully. Books and words need to be appropriate for their age level, and ones that they can see immediate value in being able to read. These are issues we will discuss in more detail in Chapters 4 and 5.

Stage 2/Confirmation: Readers in this stage are becoming fluent in dealing with print. Chall refers to this process as "ungluing" — becoming less and less dependent on having to sound out each word, allowing more and more attention to be focused on the meaning of what has been read. Rate of reading increases steadily for children who move through this stage without difficulty. Also, by the end of Stage 2, children are able to read and understand about 3,000 words, while about 9,000 words can be understood when heard.

We find that about one out of eight of our students is still functioning at this stage of reading development. Their reading rate is very slow, and the grade level of text difficulty which they are able to read *fluently* often lags several years behind the grade level which they can read *accurately*. As a result, reading becomes a task to avoid, one that brings very little pleasure or satisfaction while doing it. For this reason, teachers of older students in this stage of reading development need to take great care in selecting reading materials that make the effort required on the part of the reader worthwhile.

Stage 3/Reading to Learn: This stage marks a transition from a focus on learning how to read to an emphasis on using reading as a tool for learning new information. Readers in this stage are able to decode in a more or less automatic way. As such, they may be able to read words for which they do not know the meaning. Adolescents in this stage of reading development may also begin to encounter words that, although not totally new, are not totally known. Without a teacher's help, confusion and frustration can result, and interest and motivation can soon fade away.

About one out of every two teens we have worked with has been in Stage 3 of reading development. They have no familiarity with some words, because of limitations in their knowledge bases. They may recall seeing or hearing other words, but they are unable to separate the meanings of the words from the contexts in which they have encountered them. They end up getting caught in a vicious cycle: Their weak vocabularies cause their comprehension to suffer, and their difficulties in comprehension cause their vocabularies to remain weak. Breaking the cycle will usually require systematic, continuous, and direct vocabulary instruction. For more details on effective approaches to vocabulary instruction, see Chapter 6.

Stage 4/Multiple Viewpoints: Students in Stage 4 are able to read and understand a broad range of materials. Still developing, however, is their ability to integrate the different viewpoints and perspectives they experience through their reading. They are also in the process of acquiring the ability to use a number of different sources of reading materials as a way to answer questions and to solve problems.

Based on current educational practice, Stage 4 reading usually develops during high school. Consequently, nearly all of the students with whom we work benefit from some assistance in learning how to use the study skills and strategies necessary to organize and assess the multiplicity of viewpoints that reading at Stage 4 requires.

Stage 5/Construction and Reconstruction: Stage 5 readers are able to use reading for their personal and professional needs in such a way that their prior knowledge gets synthesized and analyzed by what they read.

Few adolescents, whether they are at Boys Town or not, have reached Stage 5 reading. According to Chall, getting to this stage may be the most difficult transition of all, because it depends on broad knowledge of the content being read, a high degree of efficiency in reading it, and the courage and confidence to form an opinion.

Thinking about reading development in terms of stages has helped us to conceptualize what has failed to develop, what has developed differently, and most importantly, what still needs to be developed in older adolescents who are reading below grade level.[7]

To illustrate how a stage model has helped, consider Chrissy, 15 years old and in the ninth grade when she came to Boys Town. Chrissy was experiencing a great deal of difficulty in understanding what she read. But teaching her different kinds of strategies for improving her comprehension skills wasn't

---

[7] See also Roswell and Chall's (1994) discussion of how reading stages can be used to understand the causes and treatment of reading difficulties.

helping her to improve. Why? Because Chrissy was a Stage 2 reader. She read very slowly (about 100 words per minute at the fifth-grade level), and to compensate for her slow reading rate, she would guess at words rather than take the time and effort to decode them. For example, she would say "calendar" for *cylinder*, or "efficiently" for *effectively*. It's not too difficult to imagine how guesses like that affected her understanding of what she read! Before Chrissy could become a better comprehender, she needed to become more fluent in her word recognition skills. Lack of automaticity was the *source* of her reading problem; poor comprehension was the *consequence*.[8]

Many times, remedial reading teachers, particularly those working with teenagers, can feel overwhelmed by the reading needs of their students. Some teachers try to address every reading need, spreading their instruction so thin that it never seems to them that they get anything accomplished. Other teachers opt not to teach reading at all, preferring instead to provide students with ways to cope with their reading problems.

With the benefit of a developmental approach to understanding reading difficulties, we have been able to accelerate our students' reading growth by focusing our instruction only on the knowledge and skills that are most critical for moving them to their next stage of reading development.

A necessary step in doing this is identifying students' current level of reading development. The procedure we use is presented in the next chapter.

---

[8] See Perfetti (1985), Stanovich (1986), and Spear-Swerling and Sternberg (1996) for a review of the research on the relationship between fluent word recognition and comprehension.

Chapter 3

Identifying Reading Strengths and Needs

Within a week of their arrival at Boys Town, each youngster is tested individually using the *Diagnostic Assessments of Reading* (DAR) test (Roswell & Chall, 1992). The DAR is a criterion-referenced test which can be used to establish mastery levels (ranging from the first- through twelfth-grade levels) in six areas of reading and related language skills: word recognition, oral reading of connected text, knowledge of word meanings, silent reading comprehension, spelling, and word analysis.[9]

Word recognition subtest: used to evaluate students' ability to identify words. The subtest contains graded lists of words of increasing levels of difficulty, and an individual's score is the highest grade level at which 70% or more of the words are read accurately. In addition to a grade level score on the word recognition subtest of the DAR or a test like it,[10] analysis of students' errors also can provide some important information about their skills in word identification.

For instance, take Sheila, one of the students mentioned in Chapter 1. When she encountered words not immediately familiar to her, she would start by sounding them out. But then she would substitute a word that began the same way (e.g., she said "consideration" for *concentration*). Other students try to sound the words out, but make errors because they apply phonetic knowledge incompletely (e.g., they might say "here-ick" for *heroic*). Still others apply their phonics knowledge correctly, but end up mispronouncing a word because they are unfamiliar with it (e.g., they will say "com-promise" for *compromise*). When working with older students, knowing how they approach word recognition can be as useful as knowing which words they can read.

---

[9] Chall and Curtis (1990) describe other tests that can be used to gather the same kinds of diagnostic information. We prefer the DAR at Boys Town because of its ease in administration, scoring, and interpretation, as well as the convenience of having all the subtests together in one test.

[10] The *Brigance Diagnostic Inventory of Essential Skills* (Brigance, 1980), the *Wide Range Achievement Test-3* (Wilkinson, 1993), and the *Woodcock-Johnson Psychoeducational Battery-Revised* (Woodcock & Johnson, 1989) are all tests that can be used.

Oral reading subtest: used to assess students' accuracy in reading words in context. Using graded text selections of increasing difficulty, the examiner gives the DAR to establish the highest grade level at which an individual can read a selection aloud with 95% accuracy.[11]

As with the word recognition subtest, we analyze the frequency and kinds of oral reading errors made by students. For instance, if students are substituting words while they read, do the substitutions make sense in the context of the passage? Are students pausing at phrase and sentence boundaries? How does their performance on this subtest compare to their performance on the word recognition subtest? Frequently we find that when students' word recognition is better in context than in isolation, they are using context to compensate for poor word analysis and/or word recognition skills.

To estimate students' reading fluency, we also record their oral reading rate. Typically, by the end of fifth grade, children are reading aloud from grade-appropriate materials at a rate of about 130 words per minute.[12] At Boys Town, the average rate for incoming youth is only 100 words per minute. In fact, a number of our students read so slowly that, by the time they reach the end of a sentence, they cannot remember how the sentence began! For students like these, increasing reading enjoyment and improving comprehension will depend on improving reading rate.[13]

Word meaning subtest: used to measure the extent of students' knowledge about the meanings of words. The subtest contains graded word lists of increasing difficulty. The examiner presents the words orally, and the student's score on the DAR is the highest grade level at which 80% or more of the words can be defined correctly. Because the DAR uses a verbal presentation, it resembles a language test[14] or an intelligence test[15] more than it does a reading test.

This subtest reveals one of the greatest deficits among our incoming youth: insufficient knowledge of word meanings and concepts. About 40% of our teens perform at least two years below their grade level in school on this subtest.

---

[11] Tests like the *Gray Oral Reading Test-3* (Wiederholt & Bryant, 1992) and the *Durrell Analysis of Reading Difficulty* (Durrell & Catterson, 1980) give similar information.

[12] See Hasbrouck and Tindal, 1992.

[13] Bristow and Leslie (1988) have made a similar observation about the reading rates of adults with reading difficulties.

[14] For example, see the *Comprehensive Receptive and Expressive Vocabulary Test* (Wallace & Hammill, 1994).

[15] See the *Wechsler Intelligence Scale for Children* (Wechsler, 1991) as an example.

For the majority, poor vocabularies are most likely the consequence of not having done much reading. By late adolescence, however, the situation has turned into a "Catch-22"; because their vocabularies are weak, their comprehension suffers. But because their comprehension suffers, little new information can be gained when they read. Consequently, for many older teens with reading difficulties, direct vocabulary instruction may be the optimal program.[16]

Reading comprehension subtest: used to evaluate students' skills in silent reading. Graded selections of increasing difficulty are presented to students to read silently first and then answer multiple-choice comprehension questions (with the text present). An individual's score on the DAR is the highest grade level at which 75% of the questions can be answered correctly. For an even richer picture of students' comprehension abilities, they can be asked to give an oral summary of the text selections.[17]

About one-third of our students perform more than two years below their grade level in comprehension. Factual and main idea questions seem to cause the most difficulty; problems in summarizing are common as well. But, we also find that nearly half of our incoming students are able to read and understand materials at, or close to, their grade level in school. Testing the students individually — with an untimed format — may help to enhance their performance on this subtest. Even so, such a result calls into question the widespread belief that failure to understand is at the root of school failure for most troubled youth, and challenges us to seek other sources for the learning problems encountered by many at-risk teenagers.[18]

Spelling: used to assess written word knowledge. This subtest contains graded lists of increasingly difficult words, and an individual's score is the highest grade level at which 80% or more of the words are spelled correctly.[19]

Incoming youth at Boys Town have great difficulty with spelling, and since

---

[16] Our vocabulary results are consistent with a study by Chall, Jacobs and Baldwin (1990) of the development of reading and writing among low-income children. Although they had adequate intelligence, the vocabularies of the students in the Chall study began to decline at about fourth grade. By the seventh grade, the children had fallen more than two years behind.

[17] The *Diagnostic Reading Scales* (Spache, 1981) or the *Standardized Reading Inventory* (Newcomer, 1986) can be administered in a similar way.

[18] Wehlage and his colleagues (1989) found a similar result: "Although we found literal inability to do the work a relatively rare characteristic of at-risk students, it is the case that increased time and more intensive tutoring were required for many" (p. 124).

[19] The *Test of Written Spelling-2* (Larsen & Hammill, 1986) is another test that can be used.

they must fill out forms as part of their admission process, spelling is often the first indication that they have a reading problem. When this subtest from the DAR is administered, one out of every two students scores two years or more below grade level. Many of the students do not even spell well enough for a spell-checker to make a suggestion about the word they are trying to write.

In addition to their grade-level score, analyses of students' correct and incorrect spellings tell us a great deal about their facility with letter-sound relationships, as well as the strategies they use when approaching words. For instance, Sheila wrote "vioces" for *voices*, and "isanld" for *island*, suggesting that she needed to learn how to combine her knowledge about the way words look with knowledge about the way they sound. Other errors indicate that students may benefit from more attention to the meanings of the words they are spelling. For instance, a student who writes "goverment" for *government* can usually correct the error when asked to think about the verb form (*govern*).

In general, we have found that focusing first on what is *right* about students' spelling errors gives us a good start on figuring out how to help them fix what is wrong.[20]

Word analysis subtest: used to estimate students' knowledge and skills in word attack. The DAR contains several items for assessing mastery of consonant sounds and consonant blends, a variety of vowel sounds, and polysyllabic words. The decision about which items to administer is made on the basis of students' performance on the word recognition subtest. (The *Woodcock-Johnson* can also be used to assess word analysis; the most notable difference is that the DAR uses real words, while the W-J uses nonsense words.)

With younger students, we have found that the DAR word analysis subtest results are very helpful in establishing the word attack knowledge and skills they have yet to learn. But when we test older adolescents, we have observed that even when students can readily read the words, they do not always know the phonics elements being assessed. This is so because they have memorized the words (e.g., *hat, hate*) rather than mastered the principles (*closed syllable, rule of silent e*). For this reason, with older students, we look at the results from the word recognition and spelling subtests before establishing whether principles of word analysis need to be taught.

---

[20] The importance of understanding the logic of students' errors is the basis of both Mina Shaughnessy's (1977) classic study of basic writers, and Roswell's and Chall's (1994) practical guide to creating successful readers. For specific information on error analysis in spelling, see Moats (1995).

The DAR takes between 30 to 40 minutes to administer. Nearly every student who takes it is cooperative, and most of them express interest during testing in knowing their test results. We always share the information with them. Because of the nature of the test, we are always able to discuss with them their strengths as well as their needs. Frequently, they will nod when they learn of their mastery levels, and some will even express a feeling of relief that they no longer have to try to hide the difficulties they have been having.

Once the DAR has been administered, a diagnostic report is prepared on the student and sent to administrators and counselors. (See Figure 3-1 on the next page.) A student's results are used to make decisions about which courses he or she will take, and each of the student's teachers receives a copy of the report. We find that when every teacher is informed early on about the extent of a student's reading skills, they can make accommodations right away.

Analyses of grouped DAR data also are used for curriculum and program planning. From our test results, we have learned that the at-risk youth we work with have had little opportunity — or encouragement — to handle the kind of abstract and technical language usually introduced in reading materials at about the fourth-grade level.[21] As a result, they have not acquired the word meaning and conceptual knowledge necessary to understand what they read. The DAR results have led Boys Town teachers to intensify their emphasis on vocabulary in their content area courses, thereby enhancing students' ability to use reading as a means to expand what they know.

Another outgrowth of DAR testing has been the realization that some students need more focused and robust interventions than they could possibly get in their content area classes. For those students, we designed a specific reading curriculum, the components of which are described in more depth in Chapter 4.

---

[21] Recall Jeanne Chall's "Stage 3: Reading to Learn," described in Chapter 2.

Figure 3-1: Diagnostic Assessments of Reading Report

Student: Phil   **Grade: 10**   **Age: 16**

Word Recognition: 2nd **grade reading level**

He works quickly and recognizes most of the words at the 2nd grade level as wholes; at the 3rd grade level, his errors are a mix of real word substitutions and nonwords.

Oral Reading: 4th **grade reading level**

He reads slowly and haltingly at the 4th grade level (about 90 wpm); his oral reading errors tend to be real words that make sense in the context of the sentence, but which change the sentence's meaning (e.g., he said "popular" for *peculiar*).

Silent Reading: 4th **grade reading level**

He misses questions that require attention to detail at the 4th grade level; when asked to summarize he lists facts from the passage.

Word Meaning: 9th/10th grade reading level

He knows the meanings of most of the words at his grade level.

Spelling: 3rd **grade reading level**

His errors are phonetic in nature (e.g., he wrote "famos" for *famous*); his handwriting is fair.

Word Analysis: **Mastery on all subtests**

Overall Evaluation:

Phil was polite and cooperative during testing. He would benefit from instruction in advanced letter-sound correspondences (via phonics and spelling). Practice in oral reading to promote accuracy and fluency in word recognition will improve his comprehension.

Chapter 4

Components of Effective Reading Instruction

In the process of designing a reading curriculum for adolescents, Reading Center staff made a list of the factors that we knew would be necessary to make our instruction effective. In this chapter, we share that list, along with how we attempted to address each component in our instruction.[22]

Instruction must be based on theory and research

When we talk with colleagues about the way we teach reading, they frequently ask: "But what's *new* about what you're doing?" The question always surprises us. Our intent was never to make up something new. We needed to design something that would work. This had two influences on how we developed and refined our curriculum. First, we drew as much as we could from existing reading theory and research. (See Chapter 3.) And second, we watched as closely as we could the progress that our students were making as they proceeded through the program.

From the outset, teachers and students told us positive things. "When I first started, I couldn't even read a whole paragraph and now I can," one student remarked. One of the teachers said: "I can think of students in the past who walked in the first day and said 'I don't read.' I say to them, 'In this class, we all read.' By the time the semester ends, there's no hesitation. They volunteer to read. They want to read right away. And they want to read more."

These kinds of testimonials made us feel that we were on the right track, but we wanted other kinds of evidence of student growth. One approach we used was to follow 40 Boys Town students as they proceeded through the curriculum, testing them as they began the reading program, and then again at the end of each of four semesters.

We used the Basic Reading and Vocabulary subtests from the *Woodcock-Johnson Psycho-Educational Battery*, one of the most widely used reading assess-

---

[22] Many of the points made in this chapter first appeared in Curtis and Longo (1997).

ments.[23] On average, students gained more than a year in reading achievement for every semester's worth of instruction. In Basic Reading, the mean grade equivalent went from 3.6 to 8.8; in Vocabulary, it went from 4.9 to 9.7.

We also tested the students' spelling, using the *Wide Range Achievement Test*. Gains were more moderate (from a mean grade equivalent of 3.2 to 5.7 over the two-year period); however, the words students misspelled at the end of the program were much closer to the actual words they were trying to spell than they were at the beginning.

In another study, we administered the *Stanford Diagnostic Reading Test* (Karlsen & Gardner, 1985). On the Vocabulary subtest, students' mean grade equivalent went from 6.9 to 8.4 during their second year in the program (n=74); scores on the Comprehension subtest went from 5.5 to 6.9 (n=45).

Although these results were very encouraging, we wondered whether students in a public high school setting could make as much progress as the Boys Town students did. An area high school agreed to collaborate with us on the project, and 16 students, all reading below the fourth-grade level, began the program. About half of the students were special education students, and about half were in regular education. A teacher at the school was trained to deliver the instruction, and we used the same measures as we did with the Boys Town youth.

By the end of two years, 12 of the students were still enrolled in the program, a finding that impressed the school administrators. Moreover, we found that gains in reading were similar to those we had observed at Boys Town. W-J Basic Reading scores went from a mean of 3.7 to 9.2; W-J Vocabulary, from 6.0 to 11.0; WRAT Spelling, from 4.5 to 7.0; SDRT Vocabulary, from 5.3 to 8.1; SDRT Comprehension, from 5.0 to 6.5.

Over the years we have continued to monitor the progress of the students participating in our curriculum, both on Boys Town's campus and elsewhere. Based on our experiences, the following questions help us to establish how well our program works: Is it worthwhile? (Do students and teachers see value in doing it?) Is it effective? (Are students experiencing accelerated reading growth?) Can it be replicated? (When others use it, do they get the same results?)

If teachers at any of the sites with whom we work answer "No" to these questions, we return to step one. Are they drawing as much as they can from existing theory and research? Over time, program "drift" can occur, and teachers can lose sight of the theoretical and research bases for their practices. Dur-

---

[23] See Stewart, Reynolds, and Lorys-Vernon (1990).

ing follow-up consultation, we stress this concept: Making it work doesn't require making it up!

Focus must be on appropriate knowledge and skills

When a curriculum has a strong foundation in theory and research, students are continuously engaged in tasks that are at the appropriate level of their reading development.

In our program, we try to focus only on the skills and knowledge that are necessary for moving our students to the next stage of development. For adolescents reading at the lowest levels, we focus on acquisition and application of word analysis skills, followed by the development of fluency in recognizing words and their meanings.[24] For adolescents at more intermediate reading levels, we provide direct instruction of new words, concepts, and ideas, and include opportunities to read and react to texts that contain this new information.[25] And for adolescents at more advanced reading levels, we focus instruction on tasks that require wide reading and use of reading and writing as tools to integrate information and solve problems.[26]

Focusing on appropriate knowledge and skills also requires building on a student's strengths to meet his or her needs. Take Mark, for example. Mark was 16 years old, and a tenth-grader in a public high school when he began our program. Although he had difficulty reading text above the third-grade level, his vocabulary knowledge was at about the seventh- to eighth-grade levels. He struggled during instruction and practice in word recognition. However, his teacher was able to interest Mark enough in the content of what he was reading to make that struggle worthwhile. Later, when we asked him what he would say to other students entering the program, Mark said, "No matter how hard the work is, just stick with it. The courses are helpful. People making me read made me read better because I got *used* to reading words."

Instruction should be structured and planned

For anyone who has failed in school, an environment where expectations are stated clearly and risk-taking is encouraged is crucial. This is particularly true

---

[24] Chall's Stages 1 and 2.

[25] Chall's Stage 3.

[26] Chall's Stage 4.

for adolescents. When teens know ahead of time what they will be asked to do, and that help will be available when they need it, they feel safe and in control.[27] A program also must make sense to them, and provide them with hope. They need to know why they have been placed in a particular course of instruction, and more importantly, what they will be able to do when they complete it. In Chapter 9, we will discuss classroom management in more detail, along with the effects that planning and structure can have on students' behaviors.

Teaching materials and techniques need to be age-appropriate

One of the difficulties in teaching older students to read is that many of the methods and materials available are designed for younger kids, and will often look "babyish" to teens. Even when materials look mature, the content included may be written at too low a level of difficulty to produce growth.

We found that out when we tried the *Laubach Way to Reading* program with some of our students.[28] Laubach, like many beginning reading programs, teaches the relationship between letters and sounds with high frequency, predictable words. (For instance, to teach the "oa" sound, words like *oat* and *boat* are used.) Since our students could already read those words, the Laubach materials were not challenging enough to allow them to extend and apply the information they were learning.

In order for teens to have the opportunity to generalize and to see value in the instruction they are receiving, materials must be difficult enough to offer them continual challenge. In the case of the lowest level readers, word analysis is best taught with words whose meanings are known, but which cannot be read. (For example, to teach "oa," we use words like *boast, charcoal, cockroach, scapegoat.* See Chapter 5 for more detail.) In the case of the highest level readers, this means providing activities that require them to apply the information-processing strategies they are learning in stimulating ways.

When we begin a training session with teachers, their first reaction often is that our methods and materials are too difficult, and that we are expecting too much in too little time. This certainly would be true if our goal was to have

---

[27] See also Roswell and Chall (1994) for a discussion of ways that teachers can develop productive relationships that will help students with a history of reading problems.

[28] The Laubach program was developed for adults with limited reading skills; it is published by New Readers Press in Syracuse, NY. A more complete description of our work with this program can be found in Curtis and Chmelka (1994).

students perform every task we give them with 100% accuracy. But that's not our goal. Learning is! Teachers and students need to keep this in mind. When we define success, we define it by how much someone learns, not by how well a task is performed. Suppose, after a week of instruction, John scores 75% on a test. That wouldn't be viewed as very good performance by most people. But suppose as well that John scored 25% at the beginning of the week. Clearly, his 75% is something to celebrate. When we measure students' success in terms of how much is learned, they are willing to be continually challenged. And, as challenge results in growth, their motivation to learn more increases.[29]

Learning needs to take place in stages

One-trial learning hardly ever occurs. As teachers, we don't always remember that; we tend to assume that if we said something once, the students who didn't get it weren't paying attention or trying!

A very large body of research tells us the following: Effective instruction proceeds in stages or steps, beginning with direct instruction, demonstration or modeling, followed by guided application, and ending with independent practice.[30]

We have been successful in using this sequence throughout our curriculum. For example, to promote understanding of the alphabetic principle, we teach the concept of a syllable and then model how words can be broken into these parts. Following that, students use computer software to practice the reading and spelling of words divided into syllables. Finally, students are provided with independent practice via a cloze task with syllables. (In cloze tasks, portions of words or sentences are omitted, and learners must try to fill in the "blanks.")

We have found the same general approach to be successful when teaching vocabulary. We use direct instruction to introduce definitions and examples of different contexts in which words can be used. We then give students activities to engage them in discussions to provide supported practice. Finally, students practice independently by incorporating vocabulary in their speaking and writing.

It's interesting that, although these steps have been around for a long time in education, the order in which teachers use them seems to change from time to time. For instance, we have observed classrooms where students are pre-

---

[29] See the work of Izard (1991) and Eisenberger (1992) for discussion of the relationships among effort, enjoyment, motivation, and intellectual growth.

[30] For reviews of this research, see Brophy and Good (1986); Rosenshine, Meister and Chapman (1996); Rosenshine and Stevens (1984).

sented with a task to figure out; then, if they're not successful, the teacher provides hints. As a last resort, the teacher provides the answer if students still aren't able to discover the solution.

Our experience tells us that when you work with students who have a history of academic failure, you set them up to fail again unless you start with the first step: direct instruction.

Teachers need to be trained

Few teachers get much formal training in how to teach "hard-to-teach" kids. And, according to research sponsored by the National Institutes of Health, even fewer seem to know any specific methods or materials to use when children have difficulty in learning to read.[31] Given this, it's not surprising that more than 40% of the nation's fourth-graders have little or no mastery of the knowledge and skills needed to read grade-level material,[32] and that for students who haven't learned to read by fourth grade, it is quite likely that their reading difficulties will persist into adulthood.[33]

When teachers do receive training in specific methods and approaches appropriate for use with students experiencing difficulty in learning to read, the approach is often one of "train and hope" — teachers may receive one day of in-service but never see the trainer again once they have started to implement the instruction in their classrooms.

Teacher training and consultation have been essential ingredients to the success of our reading instruction. Teachers need to understand the rationales behind curricula and the goals and principles of what they are teaching. They need to be familiar with the reading profiles of their students, and understand how the causes and consequences of reading problems interact. They also must have opportunities to ask questions and to seek advice and receive feedback once instruction has begun.

Results must replicate

Far too many teenagers in this country cannot read at all, or they struggle through school — and life — with reading skills well below their age levels.

---

[31] *New York Times* editorial, January 25, 1997.

[32] National Assessment of Educational Progress, a congressionally mandated survey administered by the National Center for Education Statistics, U.S. Department of Education.

[33] See Adams (1990); Chall (1983, 1996).

Because of these difficulties, most of them are unfairly destined for low-skilled careers in an increasingly high-tech world.

Unfortunately, not much time or effort is devoted to helping older children improve their reading abilities while they are still in school. Typically, reading programs around the country are aimed at improving the skills of children in grades one through three.[34] Work with younger children is very important; however, it does not help the hundreds of thousands of older children who need intensive help with reading and writing.

From the outset, Boys Town's goal was to design a comprehensive reading program that would work for teens throughout the nation. We believe that we are unique in this effort.[35] At present, preliminary results from schools in several states who are using the curriculum confirm the value of this approach.[36]

Having reviewed our list of components of effective reading instruction, let us now look again at the characteristics of our students and the constraints of our task. As we noted earlier, our students come to us as many as five to six years below grade level in reading, and they are with us for a relatively short period of time (four semesters, on average). To get them up to grade level in reading, we need to produce the kind of growth usually associated with one-to-one tutoring. But, in order to be cost-effective and teach them the classroom behaviors that will contribute to their future academic success, we must work with them in groups.

All this led us to come up with a four-course reading curriculum designed specifically to reflect our students' current level of reading development, along with the level to which they need to go next. The first two courses meet the needs of students with difficulties in word identification. The methods and materials we use in those courses are described in the next chapter. The third course, intended to build up knowledge of word meanings to improve comprehension, is described in Chapter 6. The fourth and final course, discussed in Chapter 7, focuses on promoting students' ability to integrate information via reading and writing.

---

[34] "Reading Recovery" and "Success for All" are examples of programs designed to prevent reading failure (Wasik & Slavin, 1993).

[35] Previous approaches to remediation for older adolescents have focused on instruction in specific strategies to address particular difficulties that students are experiencing (e.g., see Alvermann & Moore, 1996).

[36] Sites using the Boys Town Reading Curriculum are located in Nebraska, Iowa, Wyoming, Utah, South Carolina, New York, Texas, Georgia, and Washington, DC.

Chapter 5

Remediating Problems in Word Identification

Ted was abandoned by his mother after his father was released from prison. At age 14, he was placed at Boys Town by a social service agency after a series of academic and behavioral problems: failure to follow instructions, verbal aggression toward peers and adults, and school failure.

On the DAR, Ted recognized all of the second-grade level words, but failed to reach mastery at the third-grade level, mainly because he substituted one word for another (e.g., he said "traveler" for *translate* and "another" for *although*). On the oral reading subtest, he read accurately but slowly (about 100 wpm) at the third-grade level, frequently repeating words and phrases. He could not reach mastery at the fourth-grade level, though, mainly because he didn't even try to read some words. His spelling was at the third-grade level (errors included "tain" for *train*, and "fruie" for *fruit*). His definitions for words were clear and concise, but his knowledge of word meanings was minimal beyond the fourth-grade level. Comprehension was his highest score, at the fifth-grade level, and his summary was adequate. Beyond that level, however, he appeared to understand little of what he read.

The first step in improving Ted's reading was to improve his word recognition skills. Like many of the youth we have worked with, it had become easier for him to guess at the words than to read them. We needed to help him become better at applying the phonics knowledge he already had, and to teach him the word analysis knowledge and skills he had yet to learn.

Direct instruction in word analysis

Although many different kinds of phonics programs are available, those which incorporate a systematic, explicit, and direct approach have been shown to produce the best results.[37] With our students, we find that direct instruction via spelling works very well.

---

[37] See the phonic guide for teachers written by Jeanne Chall and Helen Popp (1996) for a discussion of why direct systematic phonics instruction works best.

In using spelling to teach word analysis, we're encouraging students to go from sounds to letters. Spelling seems to work well with adolescents for several reasons. First, we find that kids this age are more likely to admit that they are poor spellers than to admit that they are poor readers. From the outset, then, spelling instruction is something that they agree will be helpful to them. Spelling also appears to be more observable and finite to them; it's easier to demonstrate to them that they're making improvement with spelling than it is with reading. Finally, excellent computer software is available that can be customized to present the spelling/phonics rules that are important for students to know.[38] Computers are great tools for capturing the attention of adolescents, and provide them with the opportunity to practice and apply the phonics knowledge they are acquiring in a very palatable way.

Most of our students have a recognition vocabulary containing several high-frequency three- and four-letter words that are phonetically regular (e.g., *sun*, *set*, *cup*, *cake*). Because of this, we have found that it works well to teach phonic elements such as vowel sounds by teaching students to recognize that these words are also syllables (e.g., *sunset*, *cupcake*). The most common types of syllables (e.g., c-v-c/closed; c-v/open; v-c-*e*; etc.) provide us with the opportunity to review the most important letter-sound correspondences (e.g., short and long vowels, vowel digraphs, r-controlled vowels, etc.). And using syllables that the students can already read builds confidence in their ability to read more difficult words.[39]

During the course of a semester, we teach 6 different kinds of syllables, using words that are part of the students' listening vocabularies, but not their reading vocabularies. As noted in Chapter 4, this approach ensures that materials are age-appropriate. For instance, rather than teaching "the rule of silent e" with words like *cap* and *cape*, a syllable approach means that we can teach the rule with words like *escape*.

We give students 20 words a week, and every week begins with a spelling pretest on them. Following the pretest, the teacher introduces the rule that fits the words for the week. For example, one of the rules is: "When two or more consonants stand between two vowels, divide between the consonants to say the word." Together, the teacher and students discuss the rule and apply it while reading and spelling the week's words. The teacher also encourages students to suggest other words that fit the rule. (First names are a favorite pick.)

---

[38] We use a program by Davidson called *Spell It®*.

[39] A syllable approach is frequently recommended for older students who have difficulty in decoding (e.g., see Rudd, 1984; Steere, Peck, & Kahn, 1984; Wilson, 1988). *Megawords* (Johnson & Bayrd, 1988) uses a syllable approach to teach reading, spelling, and vocabulary.

During the week, students spend about 10 minutes a day working on the computer with a partner to complete activities that incorporate the rule and the words that are the focus for the week.

In addition to the computer, we have also found that word games are an effective tool for application and practice of the phonics rules being taught. As adolescents' reading skills develop, playing games promotes their appreciation for and enjoyment of language and literacy. Games also provide excellent opportunities to manipulate and expand their word knowledge and skills. In selecting games, it's important to incorporate the content that students are already familiar with, thereby increasing their chance of winning. Games we use each week are based on television shows and board games such as *Wheel of Fortune®*, *Concentration®*, *Scrabble®*, and *Beat the Clock®*.[40]

Opportunities to apply word analysis skills during reading

Phonics instruction should never be viewed by students as an end in itself; they must always see it as a means to an end.

Students need to recognize that the goal is to read the words on a page (rather than to guess at them using pictures or context clues). To accomplish this, we have them spend about 20 minutes every day reading aloud, in small groups, from high-interest adolescent novels.

Oral reading is a proven technique for providing students with opportunities to apply word analysis skills.[41] In our curriculum, when students and teachers read aloud, they gather together in groups of five to six, each with his or her own copy of the same book. Everyone takes a turn at reading, with turns passed among the members of the group the way a ball would be tossed to each other. During a 20-minute period, eight to ten pages of text usually get read, with each person in the group getting about eight turns at reading.

The procedure differs from "round-robin" oral reading in a number of ways.[42] First, students are grouped with others who are reading at about the same level, so there isn't any anxiety about not reading as well as one's peers. Second, each person reads very short amounts of text (three to five lines), so that even the least skilled reader can participate and not feel overwhelmed by the task. Third, once a

---

[40] For more information about games that work with adolescents, see Curtis and McCart (1992).

[41] See Allington's (1984) review of this research.

[42] Some of the problems associated with "round-robin" reading are discussed in Anderson et al. (1985), *Becoming a Nation of Readers*.

turn has been taken, the next turn can be passed to anyone in the group. A pass can be made at any point after three lines have been read — in the middle of a sentence, or even a word! Unpredictability makes the process fun, and helps to ensure that everyone is following along. And finally, the teacher participates as one of the readers in the group, providing a model of fluent reading.

The emphasis during collaborative oral reading is always on risk-taking — getting students to apply what they are learning about words and word parts in order to identify unfamiliar words. At the beginning of the semester, the teacher tells students that he or she will provide them with any words they don't know. As instruction progresses, though, the teacher also encourages students to "sound out" words that fit the rules being taught. Students are continually praised for making the effort to decode, even when the result is an error. With the right kinds of encouragement, students soon ask for the chance to figure out words before the teacher helps.

The success of collaborative oral reading depends on having materials that are interesting enough to make the challenge of reading them worthwhile. For this kind of reading, and with students at this level of reading development, we have found that novels work best. The group will stop occasionally to discuss the book, and their predictions about what might happen next. During these discussions students' opinions about what they are reading are quite evident, and their preferences in reading materials often are very different from what adults assume they will be. For instance, our students like historical fiction because they learn about the people of other times. They like reading about people from other cultures, too. They are not overly interested in books that include gangs, drugs, runaways, abuse, failure, suicide, and so on. Even when these plots are believable (and our teenage experts often tell us they are not), our kids don't see much value spending their time reading about things they already know. In selecting books, we've had the most success when we've followed this saying: *A book is a chance to try someone else's life on for size.*[43] Table 5-1 (p. 29) contains a list of some of the books our students have liked.

Developing fluency in word recognition

An important part of developing students' skills in word recognition is helping them to become less and less tied to the process of sounding out every

---

[43] We first read this in a magazine called *Voice of Youth Advocates*, published by Scarecrow Press (1-888-4VOYA). VOYA contains reviews of books for young adults, as well as articles about trends and themes in young adult literature.

Table 5-1: Recommended Books for Oral Reading

Listed below are books that our students have found appealing, and that are at the appropriate level of difficulty for working with students who need practice in application of word analysis skills.

Bearstone (Will Hobbs)

The Blizzard (Jim O'Connor)

Canyons (Gary Paulsen)

Children of the River (Linda Crew)

Death Grip (Jay Bennett)

Dicey's Song (Cynthia Voigt)

Downriver (Will Hobbs)

Escape From Warsaw (Ian Serraillier)

A Family Apart (Joan Lowery Nixon)

A Fine White Dust (Cynthia Rylant)

Flight #116 Is Down (Caroline B. Cooney)

Freedom Crossing (Margaret Clark)

Land of Hope (Joan Lowery Nixon)

Letters From Rifka (Karen Hesse)

Lyddie (Katherine Patterson)

Maniac Magee (Jerry Spinelli)

Missing May (Cynthia Rylant)

My Daniel (Pam Conrad)

A Place to Belong (Joan Lowery Nixon)

The River (Gary Paulsen)

The Road to Memphis (Mildred D. Taylor)

The Shadow Brothers (A.E. Cannon)

Shark Beneath the Reef (Jean Craighead George)

Skeleton Man (Jay Bennett)

Something Upstairs (Avi)

Summer of the Swan (Betsy Byars)

Toning the Sweep (Angela Johnson)

Trapped in Death Cave (Bill Wallace)

The Trouble with Lemons (Daniel Hayes)

The True Confessions of Charlotte Doyle (Avi)

The Watsons Go To Birmingham -1963 (Christopher Paul Curtis)

Whispers From the Dead (Joan Lowery Nixon)

Why the Whales Came (Michael Morpurgo)

The Winter Room (Gary Paulsen)

Woodsong (Gary Paulsen)

---

word. We have found three approaches to be successful in achieving this goal: use of word recognition computer activities and word games; collaborative oral reading; and independent silent reading.

In order for computer activities and word games to help develop fluency, there needs to be multiple opportunities for practicing recognition of the same words, along with a mechanism for providing feedback about reading rate. The activities also should require students to process the meaning of the word as well as to recognize the word itself, so that students get necessary practice in consolidating their decoding skills with accessing word meanings. Our students like the software program *Word Attack®* (by Davidson) for building fluency, along with games based on television shows and board games like *Password®*, *Jeopardy®*, and *Scattergories®*

Collaborative oral reading — described in the section before as a technique for developing students' accuracy in word analysis — also can be a very effective way of developing their fluency in word recognition. The process works somewhat like the repeated readings technique.[44] When a novel is read aloud, students can see that the same words and rhythmic language are occurring over and over again, much like they do in a poem. To develop fluency, materials must be at a level where students are accurate. Teachers can then direct students' attention to recurring words and prosodic patterns.

Requiring independent silent reading is the third way we have found to effectively develop fluency. Reading smoothly, without hesitation and with comprehension, comes first and foremost from practice. And yet, like students across our nation, our youth engage in little or no voluntary reading.[45] To assist them in increasing the amount of time they spend reading outside of class, we make this activity a part of their course requirements. With their teacher's help, students choose materials for outside reading, and are graded each week on this assignment.[46] Some students respond very favorably to the assignment from the start, while others need much more encouragement and monitoring before they get going. In almost all cases, though, students recognize the necessity of the activity. When asked what needs to happen for them to continue to improve in their reading, they echo the sentiments of a high school student who said, "Reading more often at home instead of watching TV."

We began this chapter on word recognition with a description of Ted, a high school student reading below the fourth-grade level. At the end of a year of instruction focusing on accuracy and fluency in word identification, Ted's scores on the Woodcock-Johnson had gone from 2.8 to 4.4 in word identification, and from 4.1 to 6.3 in reading vocabulary. His rate in reading text at the fifth-grade level increased from 99 wpm to 133 wpm, and he went from 82 wpm on seventh-grade level text to 109 wpm.

---

[44] In repeated readings, passages are read over and over again, until a criterion rate of reading is reached. See Samuels (1979) and Dowhower (1987, 1989) for more discussion of this technique.

[45] Findings from the National Assessment of Educational Progress (1997) show that, although the amount of reading that students do out of school is positively related to their reading achievement, only 32% of 13-year-olds, and 23% of 17-year-olds, report that they read daily for enjoyment.

[46] Some teachers have students give oral reports. Other teachers have students keep journals. Teachers have also used the *Accelerated Reader*™ (Advantage Learning Systems, Inc.) program as a means of keeping track.

Chapter 6

Vocabulary Instruction for Poor Readers

Although many people think of Boys Town as an orphanage, most of the boys and girls who come to us have at least one parent.[47] Oliver was one of those few, however, who did not.

The only problem noted for Oliver at the time of his admission was that he had to leave his former placement because of his age. After he was given the DAR, we gained some important information about another one of Oliver's problems. As a ninth-grader, he was able to read orally eleventh- to twelfth-grade texts with great accuracy and ease. (His oral reading rate was about 175 wpm.) But he wasn't able to comprehend what he read. Some of Oliver's teachers thought that he wasn't trying, or that he might have some attentional problems. But when he took the word meaning subtest on the DAR, he only achieved mastery at the fourth-grade level! He had very little knowledge about the meanings of words above a fourth-grade level, and for many of the words he knew, he seemed to know them more through aural experiences than through written exposures.

In considering Oliver's vocabulary knowledge and the effect it had on his comprehension, we found it helpful to think in terms of stages of word meaning. Edgar Dale proposed four stages of comprehension involved in word knowledge:[48]

1.   Words that have never been heard or seen before
2.   Words seen or heard of, but for which meanings are not known
3.   Words whose meanings are recognized in some contexts, but not others
4.   Words whose meanings are known

---

[47] From 1920 through the 1960s, the number of orphans (children without both parents) declined nationally from 750,000 to less than 25,000. Many of our youth are victims of chronic neglect or abuse. Some are "throwaway" children — kids who have been abandoned by their parents.

[48] These stages are described in Dale (1965), and Dale, O'Rourke, and Bamman (1971).

In Oliver's case, he had very little Stage 4 knowledge of words beyond the fourth-grade level. Moreover, words whose meanings he did know tended to be in Stage 3 — known when they occurred in contexts familiar to him, but meanings that might interfere with his comprehension when the contexts were new. Consequently, to improve Oliver's comprehension, we needed to provide him with vocabulary instruction that would increase both his Stage 3 and Stage 4 word knowledge.

With older adolescents, our best results have occurred when vocabulary instruction consists of an intensive program in which students process new words, concepts, and topics in a variety of ways. Teachers follow a number of principles in providing this program.[49]

Direct instruction is used to teach word meanings

Although much of the vocabulary that we learn during the course of a lifetime is learned from context,[50] for students like Oliver, this approach doesn't work. To successfully acquire vocabulary from context, one needs to be able to comprehend the clues expressed in what is read. But, because of deficits in his knowledge of word meanings, Oliver is unable to comprehend these clues. Attempting to increase his vocabulary by teaching Oliver to use context is essentially trying to use one of his weaknesses (comprehension) to work on another weakness (vocabulary). Both he and his teacher will be frustrated, and valuable time and energy will be lost.

Instead, for Oliver and other students like him, direct instruction in vocabulary can be one of the most effective approaches for improving comprehension.[51] Each week for a semester, students learn a new set of words. We have found that 10 words a week is about the right number.

As the week starts, teachers use direct instruction to introduce word meanings, and to solicit examples from students that illustrate the word meanings. For instance, many teachers introduce the words by writing each one on an overhead, followed by its meaning (e.g., *subtle* is one of the words, and "indirect; not obvious" is the meaning). Students copy this information on index

---

[49] See the book by Steven Stahl in this series. See also Beck, McKeown and Omanson (1987) and Nagy (1988) for discussions of the principles of effective vocabulary instruction.

[50] See Sternberg (1987) for a review of this research.

[51] On the *Stanford Diagnostic Reading Test*, Boys Town students gain about one year's growth in comprehension after one semester of direct vocabulary instruction.

cards. After students have become familiar with the words for the week, the teacher leads a discussion about their meanings. The focus during the discussion is on clarification of what the students already know, and what information is new to them. Students are asked to provide sentences in which the words can be used, and they are encouraged to say how the words' meanings are similar to and different from other related words. For instance, the teacher might talk about how background music in stores and offices, or smells like perfume, can be subtle. Students could then be asked to give examples of smells and kinds of music that are subtle, and examples of those that are not.

Following the introduction and discussion of word meanings for the week, students apply what they have learned by completing sentences containing the words (e.g., *Subtle ways to let people know you are interested in what they are saying include* ...). Like all of the activities during vocabulary instruction, more emphasis is placed on the students' reasoning for their answers than on the answers themselves.

Multiple opportunities to learn new word meanings are provided

So often during vocabulary instruction, particularly at the secondary level, teachers introduce words at the beginning of the week and tell students that they are responsible for learning their meanings (usually by using a dictionary or glossary). As anyone who has used this method will tell you, it doesn't work. For vocabulary instruction to be effective, students need to have numerous opportunities to use words and to receive feedback about how well they are doing in their word usage.

During the course of a week, we try to make sure that each word meaning receives at least 10 to 15 exposures. These exposures are included in discussions, games, writing activities, and reading.

For example, one discussion activity we have found to be very effective is modeled after one used by Isabel Beck and her colleagues.[52] The week's ten words are paired up to form questions (two words for each question), and students are asked to answer the questions and provide an explanation for the answer they chose. Questions take the following form (vocabulary words are in italics):

---

[52] See Beck, Perfetti, and McKeown (1982) for a more complete description of their program, along with the results that show its positive impact on students' comprehension scores on a standardized test.

Is *heredity random*?

Could there be a *consensus* in favor of a *misconception*?

Should you be *judicious* when *reminiscing*?

Is *bias* ever *subtle*?

Do *complementary* things *resemble* each other?

As we mentioned previously, students' rationales for their answers are more important than the answers themselves, and some excellent opportunities for clarifying word meanings arise as students tackle these questions.

Another way in which students encounter the words and their meanings is through word puzzles and games. One of the more popular games is a modification of the board game *Taboo®*. In this game, players try to get their partners to guess a target vocabulary word by giving clues. But for every vocabulary word, the teacher chooses additional, related words that are "taboo" — that can't be used as clues. For example, suppose that the vocabulary word is *misconception*. The taboo words could include *mistake, fallacy,* and *error*. To get their partner to guess the target word (*misconception*), a player has to think of other words to give as clues (like *delusion* or *misinterpretation*). Once students learn to play the game, they can work in small groups to come up with the taboo words for new target words. In fact, they probably learn as much from deciding which words can't be used as clues as they do from actually playing the game!

Each word is presented in a variety of contexts

Many words that students know are known in very narrow ways. For instance, when asked about the meaning of the word *ancestor*, one student told us "They're relatives who you don't see too much." Another student said this about the word *desist*: "I've heard that. Cease and desist. My high school teacher used to say that. I think it means sit down, shut up, and pay attention."

Words whose meanings are tied to particular contexts can cause problems in comprehension when readers attempt to apply incomplete or imprecise knowledge toward understanding new contexts. For this reason, vocabulary instruction should provide students with a number of different contexts in which words can occur in order to be effective.

We vary context in several ways in our program. One way is through the use of cloze sentences and paragraphs, where students need to figure out which of their vocabulary words fit best into blanks in sentences, based on their understanding of the words' meaning and the contextual information available. For example, for *misconception*, a cloze sentence would be: *A common* _____ *is that whales are fish because they live in water.*[53]

Another way that works well in providing multiple contexts for word meanings is to have students read and respond to informational articles. Every week, teachers give students three or four magazine-like texts that are related to the vocabulary words for the week.[54] For instance, the articles might include a discussion about the relative contributions of heredity and environment, a summary of research which shows an increase in physical similarities in married couples, and a description of how birds navigate. Each article contains at least one of the week's vocabulary words, and students are encouraged to be on the lookout for those words as well as others from past weeks. For each article, we write a discussion question that incorporates one or more of the vocabulary words (e.g., "Before you read this article, what *misconceptions* did you have about this topic?" or "Do you agree with Dr. Zajonc's explanation about why married couples *resemble* each other? Why or why not?"). After reading the article, students respond to the questions, sometimes orally or in writing, sometimes individually or as a group activity.

The "read and respond" activity is a popular one with students, providing them with their own contexts for the words (through the reader response) along with the context provided by the author of the article.

Word meanings are processed in active and generative ways

In order for vocabulary instruction to improve students' comprehension, emphasis needs to be placed on students' ability to use the words as well as to recognize their meanings.[55] We have done this in a number of different ways.

Much of our class time during vocabulary instruction is spent in oral discussion of words and their meanings. Outside of class, students are required to do a great deal of writing that incorporates the words and their meanings. For example, students are assigned a different topic for writing every week and are required to use at least five of their vocabulary words in responding. Some

---

[53] The *Townsend Press Vocabulary Series* (Townsend Press, 1997) and *Vocabulary Connections* (Steck-Vaughn, 1989) are two commercially available vocabulary programs that use the cloze procedure.

[54] Materials like *The Kim Marshall Series* (Educators Publishing Service, 1984) and *Heroes* (Jamestown Publishers, 1985) are good sources for these kinds of articles.

[55] See Stahl and Fairbanks (1986) for an analysis of the findings from vocabulary studies.

of the assignments are intended to encourage creative writing (e.g., "Describe an invention that you think could improve the quality of your life."), while others are intended to get students to take a stand (e.g., "Should smoking be allowed in public places?").

Teachers respond to students' writing using a four-point holistic scoring technique that incorporates criteria that have been reviewed with the students. The criteria include: writing so that readers can understand, sticking to the topic, using the vocabulary words correctly, expressing a complete thought in each sentence, using correct punctuation and spelling, and varying sentence length and structure. The holistic scale consists of the following:

4. Superior response. The writer met most criteria.
3. Better than average response, but some criteria were not met.
2. Adequate response, but many criteria were not met.
1. Below average response. Most criteria were not met.

Another writing activity involves giving students pairs of sentences such as the following:

> *It's a misconception that all teenagers prefer loud music.*
> *The public has misconceptioned about the hazards of smoking.*

Students are asked to choose the sentence that sounds better, and to rewrite the other one. We try to take the sentences requiring revision from students' own work so that class discussion time for this activity is focused as closely as possible on the state of their current word-meaning knowledge.[56]

Games also play a role in helping students process word meanings in active and generative ways. One activity that works particularly well in this regard is "The Conversation Game."[57] The teacher forms two teams of students and passes out three different vocabulary words to every member of each team. The teacher then begins a "conversation" with the class, saying a sentence or two to introduce a topic (e.g., "I wonder what the world is going to be like in the year 2010. Will schools and workplaces still function in the same ways that we're used to, or will everything be different?"). Students raise their hands to participate in the conversation, using their vocabulary words as they do (e.g., "I think that we'll see a lot of *innovations* in the field of medicine, like maybe

---

[56] Mary D'Angelo, a teacher at Boys Town High School, designed this activity.

[57] This game was created by Larry Thompson when he taught at Boys Town High School.

a vaccine to prevent the common cold."). The teacher judges whether students have used their words appropriately, and the first team to use all of its words wins the game.

One final activity that has helped our students improve their ability to use words beyond the classroom is one we call "Word Watching."[58] In Word Watching, students report "sightings" of their vocabulary words in newspapers and magazines, on television, in their homes, in their other classes, and so on. Points are awarded for sightings, and students keep track of their points throughout the course. Students also can receive points for using the vocabulary words outside of class, both in writing and in speaking.

Over the course of a semester of vocabulary instruction, we cover about 160 words and their meanings. Given that the English language includes upwards of 100,000 distinct word meanings, our effort may not seem like much![59] However, the kind of intensive vocabulary instruction we have been describing can yield so much more than just knowledge of the meanings of the words being taught. Students' awareness of words and their use of strategies in dealing with words they do not know increase significantly. They see the importance of a wider vocabulary, and become more motivated to increase their vocabularies on their own. And perhaps most importantly, they begin to believe that their difficulty in comprehension is not permanent, and that with effort, it can be overcome.

Recall Oliver, the student whose story we told at the beginning of this chapter. By the end of one semester in a vocabulary course, Oliver's grade equivalents on the Stanford Diagnostic Test had risen from 5.7 to 7.0 on the vocabulary subtest, and from 6.0 to 7.7 on the comprehension subtest. His biggest gain occurred in the area of inferential comprehension, where he went from 5.3 to 10.3.

---

[58] This is a variant of an activity first used by Beck and her colleagues, called "Word Wizard."

[59] This is an estimate provided by Nagy and Anderson (1984).

Chapter 7

Teaching Comprehension and Study Skills

Ann was a 14-year-old ninth-grader when she was placed at Boys Town by her caseworker. She had to be removed from her home because she was the victim of sexual abuse. Other problem behaviors at the time of her referral included suicidal statements and gestures, problems with anger control, and poor school performance. Like all students who have had thoughts about suicide, Ann signed a contract when she arrived agreeing not to harm herself. She also promised to talk with someone if she felt that she might want to hurt herself.

On the DAR, Ann's strengths included an ability to recognize words, both in and out of context, and a knowledge of the meanings of words. She demonstrated a deficit in comprehension, however, by missing an inferential question at the sixth-grade level, and missing about half of all the questions for the passages at the seventh- through tenth-grade levels. When asked to summarize, Ann's response was very general, leaving out much of the important information in the sixth-grade passage.

For students like Ann, our goals in reading instruction are threefold. First, we want to help students recognize those situations in which they are having difficulties in comprehension,[60] and to provide them with strategies to remedy the situation. We do that by teaching study skills. Improving a student's ability to take notes, make an outline, and summarize often can be the key to helping him or her become better at comprehending and learning from what is read.[61] Second, we want to teach them to be better problem-solvers. Efficient problem-solving during reading depends on accurate information. Too frequently, older adolescents with reading difficulties have given up on trying to analyze problems and gather information. They just respond. And third, we want to help students to see that reading

---

[60] Knowing when things you are reading don't make sense has been referred to as "metacognitive awareness." Many adolescents with reading problems have difficulties in this area. (See Anderson and Roit, 1993.)

[61] As Irwin (1986) points out, anytime a student makes a decision to use a specific technique to improve understanding and remembering, that student is making a metacognitive decision.

and writing are connected activities that will improve their thinking and learning. Adolescents often view composing and comprehending as "stuff" we want them to do; our goal in this class is to convince them that reading and writing can have some value for them as well.

Study skills

In teaching study skills, we usually begin with the following point: There is a difference between *topics* (what authors write about) and *main ideas* (what authors have to say about those topics). We find that many students (and some teachers) fail to recognize this distinction, and this causes difficulty in understanding and learning from what is being read. To help students get comfortable with identifying topics and main ideas, teachers may need to model the process of finding both in short articles, and then have students practice the process themselves.

We also find it important to emphasize two other points: that study skills (1) have different functions, and (2) are tools that can be used during both reading and writing. Readers take notes to hold onto information they may need to know; writers take notes to save information they may want to tell others. Readers outline so that they can easily see what an author is saying; writers outline so that they have easy access to the content they want to cover. Readers summarize in order to remember the important points that an author has made about a topic; writers summarize so that they can help readers get the important points they have made about a topic.

Once students are aware of the similarities and differences among the purposes served by study skills, "mini-lessons" can be used to introduce variants of each skill.[62] For instance, for note-taking, teachers can introduce techniques such as the Cornell, or "two-column," procedure.[63] In the Cornell system, students are taught to divide their notebook pages into two columns. They use one column to record notes, and the other column to reduce their notes to keywords and phrases. Mapping, hierarchies, and other kinds of graphic organizers can be demonstrated for outlining.[64] Mapping involves making a

---

[62] By mini-lessons, we mean brief, focused segments of class time where teachers explain and/or demonstrate concepts and skills that students need (Zemelman, Daniels, & Hyde, 1993).

[63] Created by Walter Pauk at Cornell University. Procedures for introducing this technique, as well as others, can be found in Schumm and Radencich (1992).

[64] A number of commercial materials provide excellent activities for introducing these skills. One we always recommend is Simons (1991).

visual representation of the relationships among ideas, concepts, and topics in a text. In a hierarchy, placement of the items in the "map" indicates the importance of the ideas in the text.

Probably more important than the specific study techniques or procedures that teachers choose to introduce, though, is providing practice with a purpose. Students need to be given numerous opportunities to apply the different study skills they are learning. But to be effective, the practice must take place in situations that are meaningful to students. Our students get purposeful practice in using study skills via the other two components of our comprehension program – problem-solving and question-answering.

Solving problems

Inadequate problem-solving ability not only affects students' reading comprehension, but it also results in inappropriate and ineffective solutions in real-life situations. For this reason, problem-solving instruction plays a very important role in the Education Model developed by Boys Town.[65] Every course in Boys Town's schools includes instruction in problem-solving.

In our reading classes, we have found that the *Carmen Sandiego* software (produced by Broderbund) can be an excellent tool for helping students to apply the strategies they are learning for solving problems. In the software, Carmen Sandiego leads a team of bandits who head for hideouts in various locations in time and space. The students' goal in playing the game is to track down the thieves, using clues that they unearth as part of their pursuit. In addition to the sheer wealth of background information encountered as they proceed through the game, students must use their study skills and problem-solving strategies to sift through the information and weigh the evidence presented to them in order to win the game. Students also learn how to use a variety of reference materials in solving cases, making class time spent on this activity a great way to improve their reference skills as well as their deductive reasoning abilities.

---

[65] Boys Town teaches the SODAS method of problem-solving, described in more detail in Connolly et al. (1995). SODAS stands for: defining the problem *Situation*, examining the *Options*, weighing the *Disadvantages* and *Advantages* of each option, and deciding on a *Solution* and practicing its application.

Answering questions

Teaching students to generate their own questions during reading is an instructional technique that has received much attention recently in the comprehension research literature.[66] Scaffolding — instructional assistance that helps someone achieve a goal that he or she could not achieve alone — has been offered as the explanation for why instruction in self-questioning works.[67] However, before students are able to use self-questioning to improve their comprehension, they need to be provided with numerous models of the various kinds of questions that one might ask.[68] We find that instruction in question-answering is one of the most effective ways to provide these models.

We teach students how to answer questions through an activity we call "The Explorations Board." The board consists of sets of questions, organized in rows and columns. The columns reflect different content areas (e.g., history, the arts, science and technology, and so on). The rows correspond loosely to Bloom's taxonomy of cognitive objectives, with each row representing a different category of question, and with each category of question associated with a different point value.[69] For example, in a Geography category, questions could include:

- *5 points.* What is a delta?
- *10 points.* Where is Mardi Gras held and when? What does *Mardi Gras* mean?
- *15 points.* Identify the states that developed from the Louisiana Purchase. Why has this been called one of the best real estate deals ever?
- *30 points.* Choose any two National Parks in the U.S. Compare them as to location, size, and attractions.

---

[66] See Alvermann and Moore's (1996) analysis of the experimental research on strategies designed to improve secondary schools students' learning from text.

[67] Paris, Wixson, and Palincsar (1986) made this point in their review of instructional approaches to reading comprehension.

[68] Brown, Phillips, and Stephens (1993) argue that giving students practice in answering questions will improve their writing skills as well. It helps them to articulate their thoughts before writing, and it gives them a greater sense of control over their writing.

[69] Bloom (1956) identified six levels of thinking: knowledge, comprehension, application, analysis, synthesis, and evaluation. On our Explorations Board, questions in the first row (5-pointers) require students to define or identify something or someone, while questions in the last row (50-pointers) require students to analyze a problem or defend their position on an issue.

- *50 points.* Using data such as temperature, humidity, and frequency of storms, defend the following statement: "The weather in the coastal regions of Mississippi, Florida, and Alabama is more wild than mild."

The Explorations Board is an effective technique for improving students' comprehension for several reasons. First, in the process of answering questions, students read widely and expand their background knowledge. Second, the board provides them with multiple opportunities to practice the study skills they are learning in the mini-lessons. Third, the board gives teachers and students an opportunity to interact during the process of learning the components of a variety of short-answer and essay test formats. Finally, students get experience in searching for materials that will aid them in answering questions (versus being provided with materials by the teacher and told to come up with questions or answers).

When we ask students which activity was the most difficult one they were asked to do in the comprehension course, they always say that it was the Explorations Board. When we ask them which activity they learned the most from, they usually say "the Board" again. As one young man told us, "It wouldn't have been as hard at the beginning if I had known what I do now at the end."

Remember Ann, the student we described at the beginning of this chapter? By the end of one semester's instruction in study skills and comprehension, Ann's literal comprehension score on the Stanford Diagnostic Reading Test went from a 7.0 grade level to 8.8; her inferential score went from 6.2 to 7.9. Her ability to summarize also showed some improvement. At the end of the course, Ann told us that the knowledge and skills she had acquired in the comprehension course had helped her in her content-area classes as well.

Chapter 8

Evaluating and Communicating Progress

Monitoring progress is important not only for teachers, administrators, and parents, but also for students themselves. When adolescents have experienced years of failure and frustration, keeping them motivated requires that they see their progress immediately and on a regular basis. Evaluation can and should take many forms. In this chapter, we focus on three kinds: curriculum-based, standardized, and survey methods. We also will describe ways to communicate progress to students and parents.

Curriculum-based measures

Curriculum-based measures are procedures for assessing a student's ongoing performance with course content. These measures are tied to specific instructional objectives and are usually sensitive to small changes in knowledge.[70]

Word Recognition. To assess students' accuracy and fluency in recognizing target words each week, teachers assess reading rate. Students are asked at the beginning of the week to read aloud the list of words for the week. Using a stopwatch, the teacher times the student and then calculates the number of words read per minute. The students repeat the process at the end of the week and compare their times. They often see a big change in their ability to read the words more rapidly.

Another curriculum-based measure is a weekly spelling pretest and post-test on the words for the week. We look not only at how many more words students are able to spell correctly, but also at how much closer their errors are to the correct spelling of the word.

Spelling also can be used to assess how well students have learned the phonics rules taught over the course of the semester. Students' average gains

---

[70] See Tucker (1985) for a fuller description of this category of evaluation.

on this measure range from 30% correct at the beginning of the course to 60% correct at the end.

We also give a passage fluency test at the beginning and end of our courses that assesses growth in word identification in context. Students read passages silently and then answer multiple-choice comprehension questions. (Based on our analyses of results on the DAR, we use passages at the seventh-grade level for the fluency test.) We then multiply the students' reading rate by the percentage of comprehension questions answered correctly to obtain a measure of "effective reading speed." (For instance, 100 words per minute with 80% correct would be an effective reading speed of 80, while 200 words per minute with 80% correct would be 160.) Average gains on this measure have been in the range of 25 to 30.

Vocabulary. Vocabulary knowledge can be tested in a number of ways. In our curriculum, we test not only how well students can recognize words and their meanings, but also how well they can use the vocabulary words. Students take weekly recognition pretests and post-tests on the targeted vocabulary words. Post-tests always include a selected sample of words from previous weeks so that review is continuous.

Students also are given a multiple-choice vocabulary test on a sample of the words taught in the course at the beginning and end of the semester. Average gains on this measure range from 55% correct before the course begins to 90% correct after completion of the course.

Vocabulary recognition tests give us useful information about the breadth of students' vocabulary knowledge; that is, words they know at Stage 3 of word knowledge.[71] To test the depth of their knowledge, we ask students to use their vocabulary words in writing, and score their usage by assigning 0, 1, or 2 points. A "0" is assigned for inaccurate or missing word knowledge (*The extinction in my hair made it long*). A "1" is assigned for partial word knowledge (*The weather was very dense*). A "2" is assigned to sentences that demonstrate accurate word knowledge (*The gray wolf has been hunted close to extinction*). By the end of the vocabulary course, students score, on average, 75% of the total points possible; at the beginning of the course, their average score is 35%.

We also ask students to use their vocabulary words in longer pieces of writing, and score these pieces holistically. (See Chapter 6.)

---

[71] See Chapter 6 for a description of stages of word knowledge, and Curtis (1987) for more discussion of the kind of word knowledge assessed on multiple-choice tests.

Comprehension and Study Skills. Study skills can be assessed by asking students to take notes or outline the important information in an informational passage. To score each of the student samples, we use the following scale:

Score Description
0 **Poor**: what's written bears little or no relationship to what's been read.
1 **Fair**: what's written relates to the reading, but focus is only on parts of the text; no key words or connectors are used.
2 **Average**: what's written represents an attempt to capture the whole text, but some important information is missing.
3 **Good**: what's written reflects the important information, but some details are missing.
4 **Excellent**: what's written captures the whole — both main ideas and details — and is organized in a recoverable fashion.

To assess summarizing, students can be asked to summarize the main ideas of an article in their own words. The number of main ideas included in the summary can then be counted.

When comprehension instruction focuses on question-answering, the quality of students' responses to questions can be assessed. For instance, students can be asked to compare the lives of two people who have made significant contributions to society (e.g., Harriet Tubman and Frederick Douglass). They also could be asked to give their opinion on which individual had the greater impact and why. Student answers can then be scored using a rubric that evaluates both content and form. To do this, we use a procedure similar to the one we discussed in Chapter 6. Teachers review a set of criteria with students which include: presenting relevant and accurate information, analyzing a problem or defending a position, writing a well-organized answer, writing the answer in the students' own words, and so on. The criteria are then used as a basis in the following scale:

5. The student defended his or her position and met most criteria.
4. The student included good information and met many criteria.
3. The student included adequate information and met some criteria.
2. The student gave some information, but many criteria were not met.
1. The student provided little information and most criteria were not met.

Standardized tests

Standardized tests are very useful because they provide baselines for gauging reading growth in students. Standardized tests also are useful because they allow teachers to evaluate whether students have made generalized gains in reading. In choosing a standardized test, though, care must be taken to make sure that it matches the reading components that have been taught. For example, the *Wide Range Achievement Test* (WRAT) is individually administered, requiring students to read isolated words aloud. If word recognition has been the focus of instruction, using the WRAT to measure progress is appropriate. If comprehension has been the focus, however, using the WRAT is an obvious mistake.

Another caveat about using standardized tests with adolescent poor readers involves gaining a realistic estimate of students' ability. In order for this to occur, teachers may need to give tests at students' reading level rather than their grade level in school.[72]

Student surveys

Students' feedback about course methods and materials, along with their beliefs about how much they have improved, are crucial to making instructional decisions and planning future interventions. For instance, we get students' views at the end of each of our courses, every semester. They tell us which books they liked (and which they didn't!), and which assignments were challenging and which were too easy. They also tell us how much they think they have improved, and how much further they think they have to go. As one student said, "I'm not as good as I want to be in reading. But I'm better."

Communicating progress

Ongoing communication of student progress is valuable not only for parents, teachers and administrators, but also for the students themselves. Parents of older adolescents with reading problems often have lost hope that their children will succeed in school. When they are made aware of gains, regardless of their size, parents often will become involved again in their child's education. Teachers and administrators need to be aware of progress so that they can

---

[72] See Harris and Sipay (1990) for further information on out-of-level testing.

support students in reading and also help to set realistic expectations in other classes. (For example, the science teacher needs to know that, even though a student has gained nearly two grade levels in reading achievement in the past year, he is still reading below the eighth-grade level.)

For students, communicating progress is fundamental for motivation. Students who can be shown how much progress they've made are much more willing to believe that further growth is possible than students who are simply told "Good job." *We always recommend that teachers tell students their test scores at the beginning and end of each course.*

Communication should avoid jargon and provide specific information about how students are doing in each component of the course. We have found that it works particularly well when teachers can meet individually with students at the end of each week. To facilitate this meeting, we use something called the *Weekly Grade Report.* (See Figure 8-1, p. 48.) The report is discussed with students and is also sent home for a parent signature.

To illustrate, the Weekly Grade Report in the figure is for our vocabulary course, called "Mastery of Meaning." *Recognition of word meanings* is demonstrated by students via their vocabulary pretest and posttest scores. *Analysis of word relationships* is demonstrated via their participation in class activities. *Response to what has been read* is demonstrated by their participation in class discussions of readings, as well as by written responses to the questions that accompany each article. And, finally, the *use of words in speaking and writing* is demonstrated via class participation, writing assignments, games, class activities, and word sightings.

Figure 8-1

Mastery of Meaning
Weekly Grade Report

Name _____ **Date** _____

Recognition of Word Meanings

_____　　　　You got _____% correct on your Post-Test

Analysis of Word Relationships

_____　　　　You always completed the Word Activity Sheets in a thoughtful way

_____　　　　You usually gave some thought to the completion of the Word Activity Sheets

_____　　　　Too often you did not complete the Word Activity Sheets

Response to What Has Been Read

_____　　　　You did a great job responding to the questions that followed the readings

_____　　　　I could tell you did some thinking about the articles we read

_____　　　　Too often you didn't respond to what we read

Use of Words in Speaking

_____　　　　You participated fully in our discussions of the words and their meanings

_____　　　　You usually participated in our discussions of the words

_____　　　　You need to participate more in class discussions

Use of Words in Writing

_____　　　　You did a great job in using your vocabulary words in your writing

_____　　　　You used some of your vocabulary words in your writing

_____　　　　Your writing assignments were incomplete or not handed in at all

Chapter 9

Managing the Classroom

Students with reading problems will do just about anything to avoid reading. This is particularly true for adolescents who have experienced years of reading failure and its consequences. Their repertoire of avoidance behaviors can include verbal outbursts, sarcastic statements directed toward the teacher or their classmates, and even complaints of illness. One young man we worked with asked to visit the nurse, go to his locker, call his mother, see his guidance counselor, or check with his coach every time he was asked to read.

When students behave like this, it's important to ask why. Are we asking them to do something that is so difficult that they will have little chance for success? Have we put them in a situation where they will be embarrassed? Are we leaving them "hanging" for too long before we supply an answer or assist them in some other way? Students who find themselves in any of the above situations are likely to show us how they feel by acting out.

In what follows, we describe a number of specific practices that have helped us to minimize behavior problems in the reading classroom.

Classroom organization

The physical environment of a classroom can be arranged in such a way as to avoid behavior problems. For instance, if students need to move from one part of a room to another during a class period, there should be a path that is clear of furniture and other students. Course materials need to be placed in a location where students can conveniently get to them as soon as they enter the classroom. Also, designating certain areas for different instructional activities is more conducive to helping students stay on task than making them find a place to work.

Instructional schedules

When students know *what* they're going to be asked to do, *when* it will happen, and for *how long*, they are much less likely to want to avoid the task than if they have no idea about what to expect.

In our curriculum, teachers plan three to five different activities for each class period. The length of time for activities ranges anywhere from 3 to 20 minutes. Activities are listed on an overhead or blackboard each day, along with the amount of time students will spend on each one. We find that this practice works well for at least two reasons. First, when students see that teachers follow the plan, they are willing to engage in even the most difficult tasks for short periods of time. And second, a schedule keeps students engaged in learning and allows for fewer opportunities to get "off task." With adolescents who may be as many as five to six years below grade level in reading, every minute counts!

Descriptions of expected behaviors

When teachers give students clear instructions about the kinds of behavior that are expected, students are likely to behave in appropriate ways. Imagine that you want two students to work together on a computer activity. You could send them to the computer and then deal with any behavior problems as they arise. Or, you could tell them before they begin just what you expect. For example:

> In a moment I am going to ask you to play a game on the computer. You'll have 10 minutes to complete the activity. You'll need to talk with each other about the answers to the questions you'll be asked, but I expect that you won't be talking about things other than the computer game. Why do you think it's so important that all your talking is about the game? [Students respond.] If you have any problems with the game, just raise your hand and I'll come over and help you. When you've completed the activity, record your score on your record sheet, and raise your hand. Any questions?

In working with adolescents, we never cease to be amazed at how often we get the behaviors we ask for — and how frequently we observe teachers who never ask.

Rationales for instruction

We have seen students resist reading instruction simply because they don't know why they have been placed in a reading class. Teachers should talk with all students about why they are taking a reading class, and how the class will build on their strengths as well as address their needs. Students also need to see value in every instructional activity they are asked to do. Most adolescents will work hard on any task, even if it is difficult for them, if they believe that the activity can help them to become a better reader. We also recommend that teachers share with students the achievement of past participants in the program. Older students respond particularly well to this kind of "consumer-oriented" approach.

Required participation

Students need to understand that full participation in reading instruction is a requirement, not an option. By pairing students, or letting students know ahead of time what they will be asked to do, teachers can avoid putting individuals on the spot in front of their peers. Asking students to keep track of how frequently they participate in each class period (e.g., by making a check mark each time they raise their hand to ask or answer a question) also helps to motivate them. As one public high school student told us about our reading program: "You can't hide out, and you learn."

Risk-free environments

Making progress in reading requires being challenged. This can be very difficult for students, and frustrating as well. It is crucial that they feel supported in this process. One way to do this is to let students know that you value errors. If a student who has been guessing at words begins to try to sound them out, he or she needs to be praised for that effort, even if the word is read incorrectly. For instance, the teacher might say: "Good try! You said the first part right. The word is ..."

Another way to help students take risks is to give them time to prepare their responses. We encourage students to take home the books they are reading aloud in class so that they can read ahead if they like. Assigning questions for homework the night before also helps to increase the students' willingness to participate in a discussion the next day.

One of the most successful (albeit the most controversial) ways to create a risk-free environment is to group students according to their reading levels. We acknowledge that so-called "tracking" can be harmful to students when they end up in the low-ability group and get materials and instruction that have been "dumbed down."[73] However, we also maintain that the evils that have become associated

---

[73] See Oakes (1985) and Wheelock (1992) for a review of research on the effects of ability grouping.

with grouping don't have to occur. Our own research (as well as that of others) shows that students in homogeneous groups who receive materials and instruction that challenge them will achieve accelerated growth.[74]

When behavior problems do occur in the classroom, specific practices — including the following two techniques — can produce positive results.[75]

Address concerns as soon as they happen

We all want to believe that if we ignore unpleasant things, they'll stop happening. But if students are engaging in inappropriate behaviors to get our attention, their behaviors will only escalate until they get the attention they seek. It's much more effective (and safer) to deal with attention-getting behaviors when they begin (e.g., "Billy, please stop tapping your pencil on the desk. It makes it hard for those sitting near you to concentrate.") than it is to wait until the behavior develops into something that can disrupt the entire class.

Treat students with respect

Appropriate behaviors in the classroom must be modeled by the teacher if they are to be practiced by the students. These include speaking to students in a calm voice, avoiding sarcasm or condescending remarks, greeting students as they enter, wishing them well as they leave, and giving and receiving compliments. Treating students with respect also means addressing problem behaviors in private. Reprimanding students in front of their peers may embarrass them, or give them the attention they seek. Either way, it's likely that the inappropriate behavior will increase. By discussing a problem in private, teachers set the tone right away that this situation will be handled calmly and collaboratively. Maintaining eye contact, using a pleasant or neutral voice tone, using the student's name, and keeping a comfortable distance from the student, all are ways to continue to send that message.

The best way to deal with behavior problems is to keep them from happening in the first place. Maximizing classroom instructional time is the surest way to create a positive environment where students feel safe and in control, and where learning is emphasized. Providing reading instruction that

---

[74] Slavin (1987) has shown that grouping for reading instruction based on ability results in better growth than instruction that uses little or no grouping.

[75] These techniques as well as others are discussed in much more detail in Connolly et al. (1995).

meets students' needs (as discussed in Chapters 5 through 7) does this. In this chapter we have made several other recommendations that can help in accomplishing this goal. They include organizing the classroom to meet students' instructional needs, planning and posting a schedule for instruction, giving students clear descriptions of what they will be expected to do, providing students with rationales for what they are being asked to do, requiring participation, and creating a classroom environment where students feel supported in being challenged.

Chapter 10

Summary

Our purpose in this book has been to describe the theory, research, methods, and materials that form the basis for the Boys Town Reading Curriculum. We believe that the following factors underlie our program's success,[76] and can do the same for anyone who seeks to accelerate the reading achievement of at-risk adolescents.

- *Instruction is based on theory and research.* A curriculum must have a strong foundation in theory and research. When students are continuously engaged in tasks that are at the appropriate level of reading development, accelerated growth will be the result.

- *Instruction is structured and planned.* For anyone who has failed in school, an environment that is clear and consistent and encourages risk-taking is crucial. When learners know ahead of time what they will be asked to do, and that help will be available when they need it, they feel safe and in control.

- *Teachers are trained.* Teacher training and consultation are essential ingredients for a successful program. Teachers need to understand the rationales behind curricula, the goals and principles of what they are teaching, and the reading profiles of their students. They also must have opportunities to ask questions, seek advice, and receive feedback once instruction has begun.

- *Classroom atmosphere is positive.* A program needs to make sense to students and provide them with hope. They need to know why they have been placed in a particular course of instruction, and more importantly, what they will be able to do when they complete it.

- *Students are challenged.* Teachers and students alike need to define success as much by how much students learn as by how well tasks are performed. When students' success is measured by how much they learn, students are willing to be continually challenged. As being challenged results in student growth, their motivation to learn increases.

---

[76] These factors first appeared in Curtis and Longo (1997). They are reprinted here through the generous permission of the National Center for the Study of Adult Learning and Literacy.

References

Adams, M.J. (1990). *Beginning to read: Thinking and learning about print*. Cambridge, MA: The MIT Press.

Allen, J. (1995). *It's never too late: Leading adolescents to lifelong literacy*. Portsmouth, NH: Heinemann.

Allington, R.L. (1984). Oral reading. In P.D. Pearson (Ed.), *Handbook of reading research* (pp.829-864). New York: Longman.

Alvermann, D.E., & Moore, D.W. (1996). Secondary school reading. In R. Barr, M.L. Kamil, P. Mosenthal, & P.D. Pearson (Eds.), *Handbook of reading research (Vol. 2)* (pp. 951-983). Mahwah, NJ: Erlbaum.

Anderson, R.C., Hiebert, E.H., Scott, J.A., & Wilkinson, I.A.G. (1985). *Becoming a nation of readers*. Washington, DC: National Institute of Education.

Anderson, V., & Roit, M. (1993). Planning and implementing collaborative strategy instruction for delayed readers in grades 6-10. *The Elementary School Journal, 94*, 121-137.

Beck, I.L., McKeown, M.G., & Omanson, R.C. (1987). The effects and uses of diverse vocabulary instructional techniques. In M.G. McKeown & M.E. Curtis (Eds.), *The nature of vocabulary acquisition (pp. 147-163)*. Hillsdale, NJ: Erlbaum.

Beck, , I.L., Perfetti, C.A., & McKeown, M.G. (1982). Effects of long- term vocabulary instruction on lexical access and reading comprehension. *Journal of Educational Psychology, 74*, 506-521.

Bloom, B.S. (Ed.) (1956). *Taxonomy of educational objectives*. New York: David McKay.

Brigance, A. (1980). *Brigance diagnostic inventory of essential skills*. North Billerica, MA: Curriculum Associates.

Bristow, P.S., & Leslie, L. (1988). Indicators of reading difficulty. *Reading Research Quarterly, 23*, 200-218.

Brophy, J., & Good, T. (1986). Teacher-effects results. In M.C. Wittrock (Ed.), *Handbook of research on teaching* (3rd ed.) (pp. 328-376). New York: Macmillan.

Brown, J.E., Phillips, L.B., & Stephens, E.C. (1993). *Toward literacy: Theory and applications for teaching writing in the content areas*. Belmont, CA: Wadsworth.

Chall, J.S. (1983, 1996). *Stages of reading development*. New York: Harcourt Brace.

Chall, J.S., & Curtis, M.E. (1990). Diagnostic achievement testing in reading. In C.R. Reynolds & R.W. Kamphaus (Eds.), *Handbook of psychological and educational assessment of children* (pp. 535-551). New York: Guilford.

Chall, J.S., Jacobs, V.A., & Baldwin, L.E. (1990). *The reading crisis: Why poor children fall behind*. Cambridge, MA: Harvard University Press.

Chall, J.S., & Popp, H.M. (1996). *Teaching and assessing phonics: Why, what, when, and how*. Cambridge, MA: Educators Publishing Service.

Connolly, T., Dowd, T., Criste, A., Nelson, C., & Tobias, L. (1995). *The well-managed classroom*. Boys Town, NE: Boys Town Press.

Cornwall, A., & Bawden, H. (1992). Reading disabilities and aggression: A critical review. *Journal of Learning Disabilities, 25*, 281-288.

Curtis, M.E. (1987). Vocabulary testing and vocabulary instruction. In M.G. McKeown & M.E. Curtis (Eds.), *The nature of vocabulary acquisition* (pp. 37-51). Hillsdale, NJ: Erlbaum.

Curtis, M.E., & Chmelka, M.B. (1994). Modifying the Laubach Way to Reading Program for use with adolescents with LD. *Learning Disabilities Research and Practice, 9*, 38-43.

Curtis, M.E., & Longo, A.M. (1997, May). Reversing reading failure in young adults. *Focus on Basics*, 18-21.

Curtis, M.E., & McCart, L. (1992). Fun ways to promote poor readers' word recognition. *Journal of Reading, 35*, 398-399.

Dale, E. (1965). Vocabulary measurement: Techniques and major findings. *Elementary English, 42*, 895-901, 948.

Dale, E., O'Rourke, J., & Bamman, H.A. (1971). *Techniques of teaching vocabulary.* Palo Alto, CA: Field Educational Publications.

Dowhower, S.L. (1987). Effects of repeated reading on second-grade transitional readers' fluency and comprehension. *Reading Research Quarterly, 22*, 389-406.

Dowhower, S.L. (1989). Repeated reading: Research into practice. *The Reading Teacher, 42*, 502-507.

Durrell, D., & Catterson, J. (1980). *Durrell analysis of reading difficulty- 3rd edition.* San Antonio, TX: Harcourt Brace.

Eisenberger, R. (1992). Learned industriousness. *Psychological Review, 99*, 248-267.

Harris, A.J., & Sipay, E.R. (1990). *How to increase reading ability* (9th ed.). New York: Longman.

Hasbrouck, J.E., & Tindal, G. (1992). Curriculum-based oral reading fluency norms for students in grades 2 through 5. *Teaching Exceptional Children, 24*, 41-44.

Hinshaw, S.P. (1992). Externalizing behavior problems and academic underachievement in childhood and adolescence: Causal relationships and underlying mechanisms. *Psychological Bulletin, 111*, 127-155.

Irwin, J.W. (1986). *Teaching reading comprehension processes.* Englewood Cliffs, NJ: Prentice-Hall.

Izard, C.E. (1991). *The psychology of emotions.* New York: Plenum.

Johnson, K., & Bayrd, P. (1988). *Megawords: Multisyllabic words for reading, spelling, and vocabulary.* Cambridge, MA: Educators Publishing Service.

Karlsen, B., & Gardner, E. (1985). *Stanford diagnostic reading test (3rd ed.).* San Antonio, TX: The Psychological Corporation.

Kellermann, A.L., Fuqua-Whitley, D.S., & Rivara, F.P. (1996). *Preventing youth violence: A summary of program evaluation.* Seattle, WA: America's Promise.

Larsen, S., & Hammill, D. (1986). *Test of written spelling-2.* Austin, TX: Pro-Ed.

Moats, L.C. (1995). *Spelling: Development, disabilities, and instruction.* Baltimore: York Press.

Nagy, W.E. (1988). *Teaching vocabulary to improve reading comprehension.* Urbana, IL: National Council of Teachers of English.

Nagy, W.E., & Anderson, R.C. (1984). How many words are there in printed school English? *Reading Research Quarterly, 19*, 304-330.

National Assessment of Educational Progress (1997). *Report in brief: NAEP 1996 trends in academic progress.* Washington, DC: NCES.

Newcomer, P. (1986). *Standardized reading inventory.* Austin, TX: Pro- Ed.

Oakes, J. (1985). *Keeping track: How schools structure inequality.* New Haven, NJ: Yale University Press.

Paris, S.G., Wixson, K.K., & Palicsar, A.S. (1986). Instructional approaches to reading comprehension. *Review of Research in Education, 13*, 91- 128.

Perfetti, C.A. (1985). *Reading ability.* New York: Oxford University Press.

Rosenshine, B., Meister, C., & Chapman, S. (1996). Teaching students to generate questions: A review of the intervention studies. *Review of Educational Research, 66*, 181-221.

Rosenshine, B., & Stevens, R. (1984). Classroom instruction in reading. In P.D. Pearson (Ed.), *Handbook of reading research* (745-798). New York: Longman.

Roswell, F.G., & Chall, J.S. (1992). *Diagnostic assessments of reading.* Chicago, IL: Riverside.

Roswell, F.G., & Chall, J.S. (1994). *Creating successful readers: A practical guide to testing* and teaching at all levels. Chicago: Riverside.

Rudd, J. (1984). *Word attack manual*. Cambridge, MA: Educators Publishing Service.

Samuels, S.J. (1979). The method of repeated readings. *The Reading Teacher, 32*, 403-408.

Schumm, J.S., & Radencich, M. (1992). *School power: Strategies for succeeding in school*. Minneapolis, MN: Free Spirit.

Shaughnessy, M.P. (1977). *Errors and expectations*. New York: Oxford University Press.

Simons, S.M. (1991). *Strategies for reading nonfiction*. Eugene, OR: Spring Street.

Slavin, R.E. (1987). Ability grouping and student achievement in elementary schools: A best-evidence synthesis. *Review of Educational Research, 57*, 293-336.

Spache, G.D. (1981). *Diagnostic reading scales*. Monterey, CA: CTB/McGraw-Hill.

Spear-Swerling, L., & Sternberg, R.J. (1996). *Off track: When poor readers become "learning disabled."* Boulder, CO: Westview Press.

Stahl, S.A., & Fairbanks, M.M. (1986). The effects of vocabulary instruction: A model-based meta-analysis. *Review of Educational Research, 56*, 72-110.

Stanovich, K.E. (1986). Matthew effects in reading: Some consequences of individual differences in the acquisition of literacy. *Reading Research Quarterly, 21*, 360-407.

Steere, A., Peck, C.Z., & Kahn, L. (1984). *Solving language difficulties: Remedial routines*. Cambridge, MA: Educators Publishing Service.

Sternberg, R.J. (1987). Most vocabulary is learned from context. In M.G. McKeown & M.E. Curtis (Eds.), *The nature of vocabulary acquisition* (pp.89- 105). Hillsdale, NJ: Erlbaum.

Stewart, K.J., Reynolds, C.R., & Lorys-Vernon, A. (1990). Professional standards and practice in child assessment. In C.R. Reynolds & R.W. Kamphaus (Eds.), *Handbook of psychological and educational assessment of children* (pp. 105-123). New York: Guilford.

Tucker, J. (1985). Curriculum-based assessment: An introduction. *Exceptional Children, 52*, 199-204.

Wallace, G., & Hammill, D. (1994). *Comprehensive receptive and expressive vocabulary test*. Austin, TX: Pro-Ed.

Wasik, B.A., & Slavin, R.E. (1993). Preventing early reading failure with one-to-one tutoring: A review of five programs. *Reading Research Quarterly, 28*, 178-200.

Wehlage, G.G., Rutter, R.A., Smith, G.A., Lesko, N., & Fernandez, R.R. (1989). *Reducing the risk: Schools as communities of support*. Philadelphia: Falmer Press.

Wechsler, D. (1991). *Wechsler intelligence scale for children-3rd edition*. San Antonio, TX: The Psychological Corporation.

Wheelock, A. (1992). *Crossing the tracks*. New York: The New Press.

Wiederholt, L., & Bryant, B. (1992). *Gray oral reading test, 3rd edition*. Chicago, IL: Riverside.

Wilkerson, G. (1993). *Wide range achievement test-3*. Wilmington, DE: Jastak Associates.

Wilson, B.A. (1988). *Wilson Reading System Program Overview*. Millbury, MA: Wilson Language Training.

Woodcock, R.W., & Johnson, M.B. (1989). *Woodcock-Johnson psychoeducational battery-Revised*. Chicago, IL: Riverside.

Zemelman, S., Daniels, H., & Hyde, A. (1993). *Best practice: New standards for teaching and learning in America's schools*. Portsmouth, NH: Heinemann.

Index

About the Authors

Mary E. Curtis, Ph.D., is the founding director of the Boys Town Reading Center. Before joining Boys Town USA in 1990, Mary Beth was Associate Professor of Education at Harvard University and Associate Director of the Harvard Reading Laboratory. She earned her Ph.D. in Psychology at the University of Pittsburgh, and did postdoctoral work at the Learning Research and Development Center, Pittsburgh, PA. She is currently employed as Director of Special Education at Lesley University in Cambridge, Massachusetts, 02138.

Ann Marie Longo, Ed.D., is Associate Director of the Boys Town Reading Center at Father Flanagan's Boys Home. Ann Marie's research and teaching experiences have included students at the college, secondary, and elementary levels. Ann Marie received her doctorate degree in Reading from the Harvard Graduate School of Education.